To my beautiful wife, Wanda, without whom I would die. Also to my Mom and Dad, Mark, Dawn, Brad and Lara, Mike Browne, Morty, Sevé, all the great folks at Y-102 (especially my friend, Helene), all the great listeners of Y-102, everyone who has enjoyed themselves at The Reading Comedy Outlet, anyone who thought the Mike and Dave Show would never last, a very special thanks to Tom Sheehan Advertising and his wonderful staff, comedian Jimmy Carrol (because he thanked me in his book), and a huge thanks to my friend Phil Schadler who helped me write some of the best lists on the back of a cocktail napkin.

Daniel Stein

Reading, PA
November 1996

(note: the dedication page was changed after my wife read the first draft)

Contents

In the Beginning 3

It's a Local Thing 8

The Differences Between 16

Jocks (Sports Jocks, not Disc Jocks) 20

Sevé the Cat 29

Marry Me 33

I'm Sweatin' Like 38

A Winner Never Quilts, and
    a Quilter Never Wins 40

Raymond the Amish Comic 45

Bermanisms 47

Holidays 52

Political Stuff 59

Movies in the Theater as We Speak 65

Y-102 and Mike & Dave 69

This Stuff is Just Plain Funny! 79

Plays on Words 89

Bad Business Names 95

Fears and Phobias 97

The Media 99

New York Post Headlines 103

Last Part 107

A word about trademarks. Registered trademarks, like Kevlar®, Kleenex® and many others, have become so much a part of our everyday vocabularies that we sometimes forget that they are the intellectual property of someone else. We have attempted to mark any registered trademarks which appear in this book with the symbol "®" to remind us all that these trademarks are the property of their respective owners. 'Nuff said.

In the Beginning

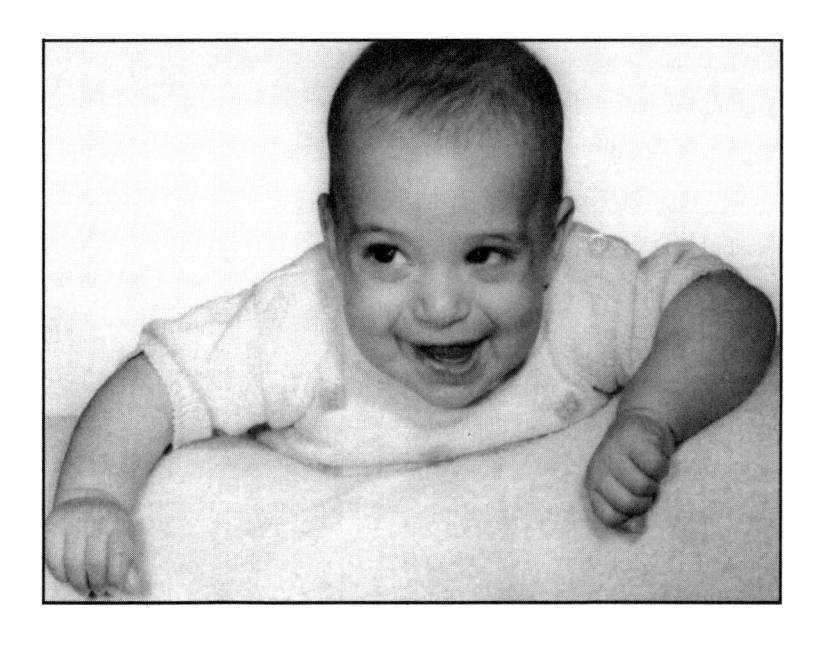

How did I turn out so geeky?

The Morning Show was created unbeknownst to anyone during a snowy weekend in February of 1988. I was working at a 1000 watt flame-throwing AM station in Pottstown, PA called WPAZ. I had gotten word that Y-102 needed a News Director. I called Mike Shannon, who at the time was the Program Director at Y-102. The Reading radio legend has since become VP/General Manager and the constant butt of our humor. I understand he's a good sport about it all. Anyway, he and I negotiated back and forth for a couple of days and bada-boom-bada-bing, I had the gig.

They offered me my own parking space, a job for 6 months and a really cool pencil.

Day One: February 15, 1988. (see picture) I was a geek. I was hired to do the news on both Y-102 and our AM sister station WRAW. That's it. No funny stuff, Circus-Boy! I knew there was a guy I was supposed to work with. All I knew was that his name was Mike Browne. So, it's 5:55 AM....I'm shitting bricks waiting to go on the air for the first time, and this huge guy with curly grey hair and glasses walks into the newsroom and says in a

Headshot: 1991
(Mom loved the earring!)

Headshot 1996

Photos: Tom Weigand Photography

gravelly, I just woke up and I've got alot of phlegm in my throat voice, "You the new news-guy?" After cleaning up my shorts I told him, yes. We then went on the air for the first time. I was shaking. He was laughing at me. Now, get this: we were in separate rooms for the first 3 years! We couldn't even see each other. All of the personality between us just came naturally. This is a very rare combination in radio.

20 minutes into the first day Mike was trying to come up with the name of a singer who we had just played. I said, "Whitney Houston?" He replied, "Yeah, it was on the tip of my tongue." Then I uttered those famous first words, "Wouldn't that be nice!" Well...Mike almost falls out of his chair. He's giggling his ass off. I'm laughing, but I'm also picturing Mike Shannon and the station GM Tom Franco running into a tree.

We simply clicked. The station hated us. The salespeople hated us. Everyone thought we were going to take the station into the toilet. Lo and behold, 6 months later The Mike and Dave Show scored the highest Arbitron ratings in the history of the station. And...here we are...almost 9 years later.

This book is based on the thousands of top ten lists I have created over the years. Let me first answer the most asked questions about THE 7:20 LIST.

Q. Where do you get THE 7:20 LIST?

A. I write it every day. (Sometimes I get a little help from some buddies. The gang at The R-Phils helped me write one once. My pal Phil has come up with a bunch of lists and topics. Recently, a group of guys and gals sitting around a dinner table drinking wine came up with one and we wrote it on a doily!)

Q. When do you write it?

A. Sometimes the day before. Sometimes the week before. Most often, though, I write the list between 6:30 AM and 7:20 AM. It has come down to the wire quite often. When I'm in the shower each morning, I begin thinking about a topic. By the time I am in the car, I may be coming up with items on the list. Other days, I don't come up with the topic until 6:50 AM when Mike asks me on the air what the list is about. It's kind of like doing a term paper the night before it's due...every day!

Q. How do you know you have a good topic?

A. Great question. If I can knock off five items on the list in the first couple minutes, then I have a good topic. Sometimes I'll have a great topic, and I can only come up with 2 or 3 items. Then it goes into the bad topic file.

Q. Who is your censor?

A. Mike. I never tell Mike the items on the list until it actually airs. When you here it, he is hearing it for the first time. I want his first reaction. However, if I think there is an item on the list that may be offensive, or should I say, too offensive, I will run it by him. He's a pretty good judge of what will or will not get us fired.

Q. Have we ever been threatened with firing?

A. Yes. I have received an official memo from the president of the company that owns the radio stations. He said I would be fired if we did any more humor about local elected officials. However, he no longer works for the company. So screw him.

Q. What time do you do the 7:20 List?

A. Yes. People have asked me this question. I usually don't answer them. I just smile and wait for them to realize what a schmuck they are.

Q. What was your favorite list?

A. Sit back, relax and enjoy 102 of my favorites in, "The Top 102 7:20 LISTS and Other Morning Show Stuff."

It's a Local Thing

State Senator Mike O'Pake and County Coroner Bill Fatora with yours truly. Hope I only need <u>one</u> of them for a while.

I've lived in Berks County for 8 years, now once. I love it. There is, however, a ton of stuff about this area that is really funny. Check out these "local" lists!

10 Reasons President Clinton Is Coming To Speak At Kutztown

10. Wants to inhale this time.
9. Wishes to take Secretary Of Labor Robert Reich to "Shorty's."
8. Thinks "Old Main" is the town hooker.
7. Proximity to Virginville.
6. Laying groundwork just in case Chelsea doesn't get into Princeton.
5. Wanted to see the Topton Christmas Putz!
4. No one at Albright voted for him.
3. Better hoops team than Bloomsburg.
2. Thought Fleetwood Mac was really from Fleetwood.
1. Thinks Crystal Cave is a dancer at Al's!

To raise money for The American Cancer Society, I had my 6 year ponytail cut off at home plate before an R-Phils game. That's Mike with the mic and Mrs. "Lorena" Stein with the scissors.

Here's a classic:

10 Ways To Know You're A Berks Countian

10. If you're pissed off already, then you must be from Berks County.
9. If you work behind a counter, and the only thing you grunt to the customer is how much they owe, then you must be from Berks County.
8. If you listen to Mike and Dave every single day but call to complain about Mike and Dave every single day...then you must be from Berks County.
7. If you double park in front of a handicapped space without your turn signal on, then you must be a Berks Countian.
6. If you ask the hooker if she accepts the entertainment book coupon...then you must be a Berks Countian.
5. If you have never been to the Pagoda, the Reading Public Museum or Christmas Village...
4. If you need me to repeat any of these...then you must be from Berks County.
3. If your dentist has to make you more than thirty teeth...then you must be from Berks County.
2. If the Boscov Department Store and the flavored milk drink, Bosco, sound the same...then you must be from Berks County.
1. If the plural of "you" is not "you" then you must be from Berks County!

10 Things If The Olympics Were Held In Berks

10. The late Gene Shirk* delivers Olympic torch via BCTV split screen.
9. Tonya and Nancy settle differences outside local bottle club.
8. 3 kitchen chairs required to save space for CBS truck outside the Geigle Complex.
7. Marbles becomes medal sport.
6. Former Gray Iron Castings building used as torch.
5. Residents would still complain there's nothing to do.
4. Olympic mascot none other than The Rubbish Ranger.
3. Olympic flag logo changed to a pineapple or some other thing flying at homes in Wyomissing.
2. Olympic slogan, "Did You Boscov Today?"
1. The Antietam School District is closed.

Gene Shirk passed away tragically several years ago. The former Mayor of Reading was also a founding father of BCTV and a longtime track coach at Albright College. This list was written while Mr. Shirk was still alive. In our hearts his legacy lives on, and he is sorely missed by all Berks Countians.

One of the reasons The Reading Phillies have been so successful has been the fun atmosphere at the yard. Former Assistant GM Todd Parnell was instrumental in bringing some great promotional nights to Municipal Stadium. I tried to give him some suggestions, but he never took them.

10 New Promotional Nights At The R Phils

10. Governor Ridge Sigmoidascope Night.
9. New Holland Night B.Y.O.C. (Bring Your Own Cow)
8. PMS Night...Just Sit Down And Watch The Game, Dammit.
7. Pat Buchanan Night...French Fries Served In Stormtrooper Boots.

6. Amish Night...First 1000 Amish To Arrive In Automobiles Get In Free!
5. Rodney King Bat Day.
4. The Night You Take Your Jacket Off..."Jacket Off Night."
3. Slow White Bronco Night...Anyone Wearing A John Elway Shirt Gets In Free.
2. Handgun And Hard Liquor Night
1. PMS Night 2...Some Lucky Fan Gets To Throw Out The First Bitch!

10 "If Jesus Were From Berks County"

10. The Last Supper would have been, "The Special, 2 vegetables, no substitutions.
9. He would have come back, but that 422-222 thing would have really thrown him off.
8. The Reading paper would have had a picture of him in the sports page with his loaves and fishes.
7. Would have changed water into Yuengling Lager.
6. Judas would have been elected to Reading City Council.
5. Some car dealer would have a resurrection sale.
4. He'd be a big Mike and Dave fan!
3. He probably would have gone to Lehigh. (it's in Bethlehem, folks.)
2. Would have to fight the Andrettis for that "of Nazareth" title.
1. Long line at the Frankincense and Myrrh Outlet.

There's no question that the folks in New Holland have gotten a ton of ribbing from the "Man Meets Cow" incident of 1995. You'll find periodic references to this in many of my favorite lists.

10 Courses Taught at The University of New Holland

10. Animal Husbandry.
9. Intro to Bestiality.
8. Remedial Cow.
7. Mooing as a Second Language.
6. Heifernomics.
5. Politicow Science.
4. Orgasmic Chemistry.
3. Learning to Take the Barn Exam.
2. Cowculus.
1. Elementary Mr. Ed.

10 New Names For New Holland

10. Heifer-In-Hand
9. Cowtown
8. Caught With Your Pants Around Your Anklesville
7. Moohanoy City
6. Tamooqua
5. Udder Darby
4. Wyomilking
3. Vealinova
2. Mount Bessie
1. The Pocacow Mountains

10 Sure Signs of Organized Crime in Berks County

10. Someone makes you a shoo-fly pie you can't refuse.
9. You find a dead fish wrapped in a quilt.
8. You get inducted into La Cosa Mennonite.
7. Now playing at a theater near you: *Ring Bologna Father 3*.
6. John Gotti opens up a chain of Chicken-Pot-Pie Parlors.
5. Bingo at church run by Sister Michael Corleone.
4. Lots of double-parked Sedan DeVilles.
3. Your bookie's name is Don Vito Zettlemoyer.
2. "The Pagoda Hotel and Casino."
1. You wake up and find a horsehead and buggy in your bed!

Remember when Pennsylvania came out with their new $4,000,000 slogan: A Memory That Lasts A Lifetime? We came up with a few slogans of our own.

10 New Slogans for Pennsylvania

10. The Meltdown State.
9. We Smelt For You.
8. The Double Coupon State.
7. Mmmm-Good...Mmmm-Good...That's the Keystone State...Mmmm-Good.
6. Pennsylvania Fever...Catch It!
5. We're Not Your Father's Commonwealth!
4. Break Me Off a Piece of That Interstate.
3. Pennsylvania...Now With Vinegar and Water.
2. Pennsylvania...Chock Full Of Wholesome Goodness.
1. Pennsylvania and Yous...Perfect Together!

With the high taxes in Reading, many people have moved out of the city, or in the case of the affluent area of Wyomissing Park which is in the Reading School District, have tried to secede from Reading. I don't get it. I live in Reading, and I love it. However, it is pretty funny.

10 Names For Wyomissing Park If They Secede From Reading

10. Muffyland
9. Beemerville
8. Lower Taxchester
7. New Voriche
6. Quebec
5. Upper Crust
4. East Volvo
3. Wannabeach
2. The Saaburbs
1. Benzylvania

The Differences Between.

Obviously, there are many differences between Reading and other parts of the world. I don't think a lot of people are confusing Laureldale and Lauderdale! For whatever it's worth, if you wear black in Los Angeles, you're cool. If you wear black in Berks County, you're Amish.

10 Differences Between Berks County And The Moon

10. It's easy to get to the moon, but god forbid you should try to give someone directions around 422/222.
9. There's weightlessness on the moon.
8. Neil Armstrong never double parked the lunar landing module.
7. People go to the moon *even* if they don't have a coupon.
6. In Berks the only 1/2 moon is when a carpenter bends over.
5. There are still hopes of finding intelligent life on the moon.
4. Neither one has a civic center.
3. If you land on the moon, you get to leave.
2. Berks County has bigger potholes.
1. The only thing that looks like green cheese here are the teeth.

10 Differences Between Reading And Tokyo

10. One has a lot of bad drivers, the other has a Pagoda.
9. They think all the Amish look alike.
8. They lost a war; we're still fighting one.
7. They can't say "L's" because of their accent. We can't say "L's" because of lack of teeth.
6. They don't own us...yet.
5. "It's Mike and Davi-San in the Morning!"
4. They have sushi. We have Sue Sheetz!
3. Our Rising Sun has a better football program!
2. They have Ground Zero. We have Ground Round.
1. They are light years ahead of us in technology. We've got bingo.

10 Differences Between Reading And Washington D.C.

10. We think D.C. stands for, "Do you have a coupon?"
9. One has the Capitol Rotunda, the other has Capitol Trailways.
8. One city is full of elected officials who don't know squat, the other is South of Baltimore.
7. One has Marion Barry, the other has...Marion Street.
6. In Washington "use" is a verb.
5. The Washington Monument just *looks* like a guy in a sheet!
4. The Potomac has $4 million dollar condos lining it. The Schuylkill has bodies floating in it. You see the similarities.
3. Washington has the Smithsonian. Berks County has a lot of people who should be in an institution.
2. Millions go to D.C. for the history. Millions go to Berks County to save a nickel on a washcloth.
1. One was named after the father of our country, the other was named after one of the 3 "R's!"

10 Differences Between Pennsylvania and Iraq

10. One's led by an unstable tyrant, the other is led by Saddam Hussein.
9. Iraq's roads are better.
8. They've got the Elite Republican Guard. Reading has D.I.D.
7. Miles of burning scorched earth. Not Kuwait...Centralia.
6. They're into ethnic cleansing. We've got a few people who don't cleanse.
5. People there wear a lot of linens. We sell 'em at 1/2 price.
4. In the Middle East, grocery store checkers ask you if you want paper or plastic explosives.
3. One has a large Anti-Semitic group. The other is in the Persian Gulf.
2. Even people in the middle east get confused over "Lebanon and Lebanon."
1. Their biggest holiday marks their founding. Ours marks the First Day O' Buck!

Jocks
(Sports Jocks,
not Disc Jocks)

Mike and Dave at the Y-102 Willow Hollow Golf Open Classic Masters Invitational. He's just happy to see me.

We've got quite a few sports fans in the listening area. Mike and Dave are avid fans. So it would figure that sports would be a popular topic for *THE 7:20 LIST.* Golf is one of my passions. With the number of golf courses in Berks County, there were a bunch of lists about golf that I thought were a real pisser.

10 Reasons Golf Is Better Than Sex

10. Usually done in a foursome.
9. A bad shot won't cause a pregnancy.
8. Generally your wife isn't with you (just kidding, Honey.)
7. If you're not good in golf, you get a handicap...
6. Someone else always pulls the pin.
5. In golf if you're having trouble on the green you can always change putters.
4. It doesn't matter "how long" but "how straight."
3. It's good if you don't score a lot.
2. You can have more than one Birdie.
1. You get to play a different hole every time.

At the Betsy King Tourney one year. Don Deeds, George Ruth, Dottie Mochrie-Pepper-Jesse-Raphael or whatever her name is now, me, Dad and Jim Luppold.

10 Reasons It Sucks To Play Golf With Moses

10. Too many rules.
9. He sweats a lot. Oh sorry...that's Moses Malone.
8. Led the Jews out of Canaan but can't make a 3-footer with a $2 nassau in the line.
7. Unfair advantage in retrieving balls lost in pond and or sea.
6. Starts out golf jokes with, "So Jesus, Arnie and I are playing golf..."
5. Expects to play from the senior tees.
4. Thinks Hebrew is one of those new microbeers.
3. Doesn't have a robe with a collar.
2. Really good out of sand traps.
1. Never gets to play The Berkshire. (OUCH!)

Of course, you can't have one and not the other:

10 Reasons It Sucks To Play Golf With Jesus

10. Unfair advantage on water holes.
9. He always gets to be Jack Nicklaus.
8. Always saying, "You know, my Dad's the only one who can hit a 1-iron.
7. Gallery of lepers and sycophants just too noisy.
6. Marks his ball with a big piece of myrrh.
5. Starts out every golf joke with, "So Moses, Arnie and I are playing golf..."
4. Most places require you to wear a shirt.
3. Does the water to wine thing but never picks up the check after the round.
2. Only wants to play Saucon Valley. (it's in Bethlehem)
1. When he hits a bad shot, he yells "ME!"

When The Reading Phillies came up with the idea for a kid in a mask cleaning up the stadium, I came up with some names for him. They chose "The Rubbish Ranger" instead. I still think mine were better.

10 Other Choices Of Names For The Rubbish Ranger

10. Landfill Louie
9. Randy Recycler
8. Incinerator Sam
7. Leachate Larry
6. Samurai Sanitation Guy
5. The Hefty Homeboy
4. The Litter Master
3. The Refuse Renegade
2. That Kid With The Zits Picking Up Trash
1. The Garbage Garcón.

Me with my favorite baseball player of all time, Cookie Rojas.
He guest hosted The Morning Show that day.

10 Reasons Baseball is Better Than Sex

10. You can still walk after 4 balls.
9. There are several ways to get to first base.
8. Sometimes it's easier to turn on a *baseball game*.
7. Foot-long hot-dogs!
6. They bring you a beer *during* the game!
5. Baseball games last a lot longer.
4. At the ballpark, someone is *always* playing the organ.
3. Your wife will let you smoke cigars during a baseball game.
2. In Baseball, there's always a chance of a triple-play!
1. In Baseball, no one falls asleep after a homerun!

10 Ways To Know You Watch Too Much Football

10. You turn up the sound for the coin toss.
9. After the game you dump 5 gallons of Gatorade® on your wife.
8. You have a catheter inserted so you don't have to leave the Lazy-Boy.
7. You start patting your co-workers on the butt for a job well done.
6. Refer to perky breasted wife as a "two-point conversion."
5. Penalize yourself for illegal use of the hands.
4. Stare at TV and say, "Coming up…*60 Minutes*…followed by *Murder, She Wrote*."
3. Bedroom antics start out with a rousing, "HE…COULD…GO…ALL…THE…WAY!!!"
2. After an orgasm your wife whistles the play dead.
1. You call your sex organ "The Granddaddy of Them All!"

Do you recall when the Eagles first had running back Ricky Watters, and he dropped that ball in a big game because he didn't want to get hit too hard? Here is the list that ran the next day:

10 Reasons Ricky Watters Dropped That Pass Yesterday*

10. Skirt was riding up.
9. PMS'ing
8. Already had broken *one* nail in the first quarter.
7. Sagging pantyhose
6. Mixed up anabolic steroids with Estrogen.
5. Mascara was running.
4. Upset his shoes didn't match his bag.
3. Didn't want to wind up on his back like the cheerleaders.
2. He...just...wasn't...in...the...mood.
1. He had a headache.

*My wife is the editor of this book, and she thought this was funny.

10 Iraqi Olympic Team Pet Peeves

10. Reebok hasn't come out with the turban pump.
9. Request to fire a scud missile to light the torch denied.
8. Robe gets caught in spokes during cycling events.
7. Even when they finish last, they still claim victory.
6. Even Bud Collins dresses better than they do.
5. Elite Republican guard didn't medal in the shooting events.
4. Mistaking Bela Karolyi with Saddam Hussein.
3. Israeli team issued Patriot missiles.
2. Always chosen last in Olympic Village pick-up games.
1. Roller Hockey chosen over Flogging as demonstration sport.

One of the cool things about our show is that I am Jewish, and Mike is Catholic. Hence we can get away with a few religious references. If Mike's Mom thinks it's funny, it must be OK!

10 Ways To Know The Pope is Skiing On Your Hill

10. The strange looking white 4 x 4 with the "Honk If You Love Jesus" bumper sticker.
9. White smoke coming out of the ski lodge.
8. The bald guy in the robe making snow angels.
7. Always has his skis crossed.
6. Still claims abstinence is the best form of safe skiing.
5. Shops at Nazareth Ski 'n Sport.
4. The only skier who won't go down the run called, "Hell's Kitchen."
3. Doesn't need ski patrol to be saved.
2. Only guy not to curse when chair lift hits him in the back of the head.
1. Takes offense to the term, "Ski Pole."

Geeks at Maple Grove. That bulge in Mike's shorts meant he would leave The Morning Show for a year.

10 Things Basketball Star Charles Barkley Has In Common With Madonna

10. Takes them both about the same time to grow a mustache.
9. Both like the same girls.
8. Both have had their heads rammed against a backboard once or twice.
7. Neither can sing.
6. Both do their best work with people watching.
5. Both have had their share of triple-doubles.
4. Both enjoy a little 3 on 3.
3. Madonna claims she never had sex with Wilt Chamberlain.
2. Both have scored in 28 cities.
1. Both have experience dodging balls in the face!

Collegeville Junior American Legion. I'm the 13 year-old fourth from the right in the second row. See the little kid third from the left in that same row? That's the guy we call "Spin" on the Morning Show. He's six-five now!!!

10 Basketball Terms and Their Meanings

10. *The Give and Go*...a quickie on Franklin St.
9. *The Pick and Roll*...what the guy in the car next to you is doing.
8. *Post-Up*...bailing out a UNLV player.
7. *Double Dribble*...you and your buddy watching a show at Al's.
6. *3-Pointer*...a chick after Three Mile Island
5. *Possession*...(see Post-Up)
4. *Technical Foul*...a really smelly mechanical engineer.
3. *Bonus Situation*...when your secretary comes in to take a letter. (nyuk, nyuk, nyuk)
2. *Assist*...that growth on your X-Ray.
1. *Jump Balls*...when a guy leaps into cold water!

The reason Mike Tyson never wanted to fight in Philadelphia was because he had trouble saying some of Philadelphia's more popular words. Imagine Iron Mike saying this list:

10 Things Mike Tyson Hates About Philadelphia

10. 2nd & South Streets.
9. Cheese Steak Sandwiches.
8. 1776.
7. CoreStates Spectrum.
6. Schuylkill Expressway
5. Lisa Thomas-Laury.
4. Civic Center.
3. The Marsupial Display at the Zoo.
2. Broad & Pattison (or any word with Broad in it.)
1. Thatcher Longstreth. (actually, he could probably say that!)

Sevé the Cat

The one. The only. Mr. Sevé Stein.

Sevé the Cat, Morning Show Personality

Real name:	Severiano Ballesteros Stein
Born:	April 4, 1989. Birdsboro, PA
Raised:	Reading, PA
Height:	11"
Weight:	15 lbs.
Disposition:	Cranky
Likes:	Iams Cat Food (for less active cats). That's it. Actually he would love some Iams Lamb and Rice flavor, but we won't give him that because he's a fat pig.
Favorite Broadway Shows:	"A Funny Thing Happened On The Way To The Vet," "Cats," and of course, "Miss Saigon Loves Dog."
Favorite Actress:	Kitty Carlisle
Favorite World Leader:	Meow-Tse Tung
Favorite President:	James Garfield
Favorite Designer:	Hartz
Favorite Holiday Character:	Santa Claws
Favorite Berks County Dish:	(tie) Funnel Bird and Shep-Birds Pie
Hates:	Dawgs.
For those who have always wanted to know:	NO, THE CAT CAN'T REALLY TALK. DUH.

LYRICS TO THE SEVÉ CHRISTMAS SONG:
Sevé's 9 Lives of Christmas

By Sevé Stein, F.O.T.A.K.*

*Friend Of The Animal Kingdom

(To the tune of 12 Days of Christmas)

On the first life of Christmas my Dad gave to me...the ball with the bell.

On the second life of Christmas my Dad gave to me...two bowls of Iams and the ball with the bell.

On the third life of Christmas my Dad gave to me...ten grams of Valium for the trip to the vet...and I don't...remember...anything...else.

On the...let's see...fourth life of Christmas I got my famanounies cut off!!! Four intravenous shots and that stupid f-ing ball with the bell.

Check out what they gave me on the fifth life...five dead dogs! A dead Doberman, two dead terriers, one dead collie. And a really dead Dalmatian.

On the sixth life of Christmas I was told I was adopted...Thanks a lot. I'll poop on the rug, power boot on the bed and bite your ankles. So shove the ball up your coolie.

On the seventh life of Christmas I found out I was half Jewish...I didn't know...Sevé Stein, friend of the animal kingdom...a member of the Tribe!

On the eighth life of Christmas I got tired of this Christmas stuff. I'm half Jewish...I found out I was adopted...five dead dogs. They neutered me without telling me, doped me up on

Valium…filled my bowl…and that mother f-ing ball with the bell.

On the ninth life of Christmas I signed a deal with HBO…they're installing it next week. Hey, I'm adopted. I'm half Jewish…half Spanish tooish…I guess that makes me Spewish! Five dead dogs! Addicted to Valium…I can't have little kitties…I can't even go outside. So I guess I'll play with the ball with the bell!

Merry Christmas and Happy Chanukah…to even the dawgs!

Here's the little asshole in one of his favorite places.

Marry Me!

I don't know why Jews do this at weddings. Maybe that's why we all complain about our backs.

On November 27, 1993 I became the happiest man in the world when I married Wanda. She's the best. She's everything. She's looking over my shoulder right now.

Some of the funniest lists of all time were the "10 Ways To Know You Married A..." lists. Example? You know if you've married a snowplow operator...he's always exaggerating his inches! Sit back, relax, pick your toes and enjoy some of the Stein household favorites:

10 Ways To Know You've Married A Police Officer

10. When you start an argument, he calls for back-up.
9. Refers to bedroom as "the pokey."
8. Secret desire to see you in a Kevlar® nightie.
7. Calls farting his "silent alarm."
6. The obvious night stick reference.
5. You never hear him say, "Oh, man, not donuts again!"
4. Refers to his winkie as "the ol' breathalyzer!"
3. Stops you in the middle of sex to ask you if you knew how fast you were going.
2. Handcuffs don't turn him on anymore.
1. Yes, that **is** a gun in his pocket.

10 Ways To Know You've Married a Y-102 Morning Man

10. Refers to foreplay as "show-prep."
9. Ask him to take out the trash...he responds with, "Thanks for calling."
8. When you're having sex, you can hear Mike Browne and Sue Sheetz giggling in the background.
7. Has to stop every few minutes for a break.

Mrs. Stein puffing on a Cohiba Robusto® at The Northeast Taproom.

6. His idea of a double-shot and your idea of a double-shot may differ.
5. Hangs up on your Mother if she's not "caller #10."
4. At home he puts on *Stairway To Heaven* every time he has to go to the bathroom.
3. Constantly checking the thermostat and saying, "Right now, it's 72 degrees in the living room."
2. Thinks he's much cooler than he really is.
1. Always yelling, "Honey...we're late. We're supposed to be there at 7:15. That's 15 minutes after 7:00."

You're probably married to Abe Lincoln if you're always catching him "emancipating." I am certain your husband is an astronaut if during an orgasm he yells, "We have lift-off!" If you are always catching your husband with his hands between some other guy's legs, then he's probably a quarterback. Your husband's been seeing a cow on the side if the new calf looks just like him. You are probably married to a sideshow performer if your mail comes to you addressed, "Rat-Boy, The Cheese-Eating Man-Rodent." You may be married to an alien if he's obsessed with Uranus. And you may be married to Santa Claus if he's had more kids on his lap than Michael Jackson.

On November 27, 1995, in honor of my 2nd wedding anniversary, I prepared a list of 10 things I've learned after 2 years of marriage. Little did I know that revenge would rear its ugly head the very next day. Here is my list followed by my wife's list.

10 Things I've Learned After 2 Years Of Marriage

10. I am always wrong.
9. If I have an opinion, I should most assuredly keep it to myself.
8. I really liked being single.
7. Wives have no sense of humor when it comes to funny stuff.
6. The pull the finger bit she does is still cute.
5. Mi closet, su closet.
4. My Mother really didn't nag that much after all.
3. I figured out what started World War II. Someone left the cap off the toothpaste.
2. She still thinks I'm a jackass.
1. I will get my ass kicked for this list.

Wanda came on the show and read her list:

10 Things I've Learned After 2 Years Of Marriage

10. He *is* always wrong.
9. I *am* the only one with an opinion.
8. Being single *was* nice.
7. I *have* a sense of humor unless he's being a jerk.
6. He farts *all* the time.
5. Su closet, *mi* closet.
4. Oh yes she *does!*
3. He looks good on his knees scrubbing the bathroom floor.
2. Why can't he aim?
1. If his penis could think, he'd be a genius.

Mike and Dave at Dave's wedding, 1993.
Beer and cigars. Why get married?

I'm Sweatin' Like

Have you ever heard the expression: "I'm sweatin' like a sheep in Shartlesville?" Here are some of my favorite "I'm Sweatin' Likes:"

10 I'm Sweatin' Likes

10. I'm Sweatin' Like A Pigeon In Hegins.
9. I'm Sweatin' Like Jack Kevorkian At The Leader Home.
8. I'm Sweatin' Like A Guy Watching His Doctor Put On A Rubber Glove.
7. I'm Sweatin' Like Susan Lucci At The Daytime Emmys.
6. I'm Sweatin' Like Louis Farrakhan At A Bar Mitzvah.
5. I'm Sweatin' Like Michael Jackson At Gap For Kids.
4. I'm Sweatin' Like Leon Spinks At A Spelling Bee.
3. I'm Sweatin' Like Ted Bundy.
2. I'm Sweatin' Like A Guy Selling Ammo To A Postal Worker.
1. I'm Sweatin' Like A Girl In Biology Class At Wyomissing.*

The Infamous "Wanging" Incident. If I have to explain it, you wouldn't want to know anyway.

Is that a fake mustache and nose? Check out how much hair I had in 1988!

A Winner Never Quilts, and a Quilter Never Wins

Amish superstar, me and Phil after a swell night at the Reading Comedy Outlet.

I like a good Amish joke. Having managed Raymond The Amish Comic for a while, I've learned to have a sense of humor about the folks in black. As Mike says, "_uck 'em. They don't have radios!"

10 Amish Sinatra Hits

10. Mennonite and Day
9. Shoo-Fly Me To The Moon
8. Sheep Be A Lady
7. Love And Carriage
6. I've Got Yous Under My Quilt
5. There Used To Be A Farmers Market
4. Ben The Knife
3. A Nightingale Sang In Bird-In-Hand
2. The Way You Zook Tonight
1. New Holland, New Holland (...These little town mooos...)

10 Reasons You Don't Want To Go To An Amish Dentist

10. Uses potato fillings
9. Open wide and say, "Baaaaaaaaaaaaa."
8. Always pulling out of the mouth some teeth, once.
7. Guy on a bicycle running the drill.
6. Anesthesia includes taking a big whiff at the Green Dragon.
5. On the good side, he's probably not playing golf on Wednesday.
4. He may have just birthed a calf.
3. Sharing waiting room with a goat.
2. Only accepts Blue Cross/ Blue Ball.
1. Office hours: 4:30-7:30 AM.

Once they found out my real name was Zook, the Amish really started to dig us. It's the humanness Mike and I possess. We don't flaunt our zippers. We both look good in a bonnet, and we've never had Harrison Ford on the show.

I really like Amish chicks, too. They are gullible, though. Next time you're at the farmers market, try these pick-up lines: Hey, babe, what's your hex sign? Come on over...I've got batteries! And, my personal favorite: My, what a lovely shade of...black.

I always thought it would be great to have a President from Berks County. He might not cut taxes, but there would be a nice coupon in the Val-Pak. He'd probably balance the budget by asking Congress: "Paper or Plastic?" Plus, the Secretary of Transportation would be Carl Bieber. What if the President Was Amish?

10 Things If The President Was Amish

10. No arms sales on Sundays.
9. The C. Everett Koop look would be in again.
8. Much lower White House electric bill.
7. No Gay Dutchmen in the military.
6. Bulletproof Schwinn®.
5. Presidential limo sporting an orange triangle.
4. White House tour now includes visit to beet garden.
3. Secret Service agents carry pitchfork and sickle.
2. We'd bomb someone and then build them back up again. (Hey, we do that already!)
1. Presidential plane renamed Air Force Once.

Historically, the Amish would have had great impact on our country. For instance, each item in The Bill of Rights would have ended with, "Why yeah, it's so!" People today would be asking for your "John Stoltzfus" when they need your signature. The famous revolutionary war quote would have been, "Don't shoot until you see the chrome of their bumper."

10 Ways To Know You've Been The Victim Of A Hit And Run Buggy

10. Black paint on bumper.
9. Real thin tire tracks.
8. Hoof prints on dashboard.
7. A lot of people standing around laughing.
6. A police chief saying, "Now let me get this straight."
5. Imprint of bumper sticker that says, "My other buggy is a convertible."
4. Harrison Ford was the only witness.
3. All points bulletin for a vehicle with vanity plate QUILTR.
2. No one got a snapshot.
1. You're the topic of The Mike and Dave show for 2 weeks.

10 Great Amish Boxers

10. Sugar Ray Stoltzfus
9. Muhammad Weaver
8. Evander Yocum
7. Jersey Joe Stubblebine
6. Eli Cesar Chavez
5. Sonny Ludwig

4. Elmer Ray Robinson
3. Buster Wagonseller
2. Gideon Marciano
1. James Bonecrusher Zettlemoyer

If some Amish are offended by any of this, I would imagine that it's tough being Amish...you know... with all the Amish Wannabees and everything. Those darn Mennonites come to town and ruin the whole neighborhood. And finally, they've got to hate those annoying disc jockeys who never have the decency to pick on the Quakers.

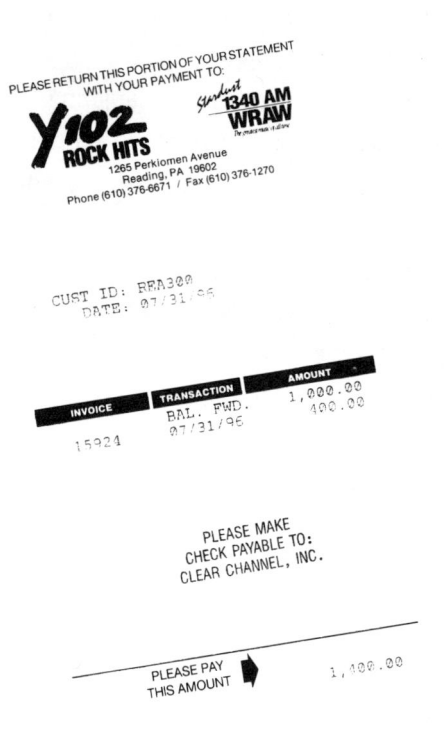

```
PLEASE RETURN THIS PORTION OF YOUR STATEMENT
         WITH YOUR PAYMENT TO:
                          Stardust 1340 AM
         Y102                        WRAW
         ROCK HITS
              1265 Perkiomen Avenue
                 Reading, PA 19602
         Phone (610) 376-6671 / Fax (610) 376-1270


         CUST ID: RRA300
              DATE: 07/31/96

                                    AMOUNT
         INVOICE   TRANSACTION     1,000.00
                   BAL. FWD.         100.00
                   07/31/96
         15924


                  PLEASE MAKE
              CHECK PAYABLE TO:
              CLEAR CHANNEL, INC.


                  PLEASE PAY        1,100.00
                  THIS AMOUNT
```

*Yes, they **do** charge me to do the Reading Comedy Outlet spots!!*

Raymond the Amish Comic

Photo: Tom Weigand Photography

Raymond The Amish Comic

Everyone wants to know about Raymond! Raymond The Amish Comic has been a part of our show for the past three years. I have had the great pleasure of becoming his friend and manager. Believe me, his friendship has nothing to do with the fact that he sells out every show!

Born:	In a barn. Duh!
Raised:	On a farm. Duh!
Lives:	On a sprawling estate in Blue Ball.
Bats:	Left
Pitches (hay):	Right
Height:	'Bout as high as a moo-cow's ear.
Weight:	'Bout yea so.

From his humble beginnings emceeing the morning milkings, Raymond quickly became a headlining favorite on the barn-raising circuit. His record of 2,130 consecutive barn-raising appearances is considered a record. Of course Zeke Ripkin, Jr. is closing in on him. Yearning for the bright lights (or any lights for that matter) of showbiz, Raymond moved to the big city, Intercourse. There, he maintains an Amish Comedy Superstar's lifestyle with a small yet stylish barnyard, a high performance buggy and 'lectric!

Bermanisms

Dancing with Mom at my wedding.

ESPN anchor, Chris Berman, has made a career out of using nicknames for athletes when he gives the scores. (i.e. Oddibe "in love again" McDowell) I think Chris is a pioneer in the sports broadcasting field. I just hope he's not pissed I use his name when I describe these lists. I look at it as a tribute. Don't you? Anyway, with the hundreds and hundreds of "Bermanisms" I have done over the years, here are my favorites!

10 Berks County Bermanisms

10. L & B Dodge's Joe Dell-O Pudding
9. State Senator Mike O'Pakes a Cake as Tasty as a Tastykake®!
8. VF Chairman Larry the Pugh, the Proud, the Marines
7. Basketball star Boris Donyeltsin Marshall
6. Golf legend Chip A Triple Lutz!
5. County Coroner Bill Fatora Tora Tora!
4. Berkshire Knitting Mill founder and philanthropist Ferdinand Name That Thun!
3. County Commissioner Glenn Reber McIntire
2. Reading City Councilwoman Dawn Step In Shutt
1. Local Aviation Chairman Mark Fruchter...I Didn't Even Touch Her!

10 Political Bermanisms

10. US Senator Rick A Funny Thing Happened On The Way To The Santorum.
9. Congresswoman Marjorie Margolis Arantxa Sanchez Vicario John Jacob Jingle Heimer Schmidt Mesvinsky.
8. Great Spiritual Guy, "Hello" Dali Lama.
7. Civil Rights Leader, Martin Luther Burger King® Whopper Jr.®

6. Emperor Haile Selassie Come Home.
5. Emperor Billy Don't Be A Hirohito!
4. Chinese Leader Deng Chow Ping Putter
3. 6th Congressional District Candidate Steve Opening Day Of Trautwein Season.
2. African Dictator Steve and Idi Amin.
1. Wacky Presidential Candidate Lyndon LaroucheBag!

10 Pro Golf Bermanisms

10. Colin Oscopy Montgomery
9. Got A Woody Austin
8. Fred What The Funk!
7. Sevé Stepped On A Rake And Hit His Ballesteros
6. Tiger Does A Bear Shit In The Woods *
5. Corey Traffic Is Tied Up On 422 Because PennDOT Is Pavin!
4. Nancy Lopez Dispenser
3. Ray Floyd's Of London
2. Ernie Oh You Never Would Believe Where Those Keebler® Cookies Come From. They're Baked By Little Els! (Long way for that one!)
1. And Finally...in tribute to Chris Berman: Chip Beck, Beck, Beck, Beck, Beck!

*We used "poop" on the air instead of shit. They hate it when you say "shit" on the air.

10 Other Sports Bermanisms

10. Baseball's Eddie Baseball Been Murray, Murray Good To Me.

9. Figure Skater Peggy Cough Up Some Flemming.
8. Baseball Player Lenny Finger In The Dykstra.
7. Catcher Sandy Remember The Alomar!
6. QB Todd SonofaMarinovich
5. Former Phillie Rueben You Say Amaro, I Say Amahro, Let's Call The Whole Thing Off!
4. QB Bernie "Who Ordered The Kosar Meal?"
3. Team Penske Indy driver Rick I Haven't Seen You In Mears.
2. Figure Skater Katarina Whatchu Doin' Witt My Ho?
1. QB Mark Had Some Chili And Now He's Rypien 'Em.

10 Christmas Bermanisms

10. NBA Star Christmas Tree Rollins
9. Civil Rights Leader Malcom X-Mas
8. Actor Yuletide Brynner
7. Iran-Contra Figure Oliver North Pole
6. From The Mary Tyler Moore Show: Ted Now He's Silent Knight.
5. NASA's Sally Sleigh Ride
4. Beauty And The Beast's Linda BethleHamilton
3. Actress Stocking Channing
2. Channel 10 Anchor Larry Candy Kane
1. Rapper Noel L. Cool J.

10 Media and Hollywood Bermanisms

10. Andy Griffith Show Character Barney Take My Fife...Please.
9. Eddie Ring Bologna And Munster Cheese
8. Actor Sidney Shit Or Get Off The Poitier*
7. Actor Robert Boy Is She Stacked!
6. Actress Laura Gad Dern Cotton Pickin' Varmint

5. Morning TV Personality Paula Zahn-fir Master of the Pan Flute
4. Sports Play-By-Play Guy Vern Cough Up a Lundquist
3. Newswoman Connie I Want a Guy Who's Really Chung
2. Newsman Tom What's Happenin' Bro-kaw
1. Channel 69 Anchor Kathy I Wouldn't Touch Her With A Ten Foot Craine!

see previous asterisk regarding "shit."

BCBOA/IAABO Tournament

Results of the ninth annual Berks County Basketball Officials Association/International Association of Approved Basketball Officials Commissioner's Tournament played Sunday at Green Acres:

Low gross official: Mike Paulson, 76. **Low gross guest:** Lloyd Brewer, 74.

Closest to pin — No. 9: Lloyd Brewer; No. 11: Bob Mastromarino; No. 13: Jim Arnold. **Longest drive:** No. 18: Bob Mastromarino.

Low net winners: Jim Arnold, John Crossan, Bob Ott and Tim Braun.

Hole-in-one

At Spring-Ford CC: David Stein, Reading, fourth hole, 135 yards, pitching wedge, his first.

For no other reason, I just wanted to see my hole-in-one in print again!

Holidays

There are worse gigs! Yes, I'm just happy to see them.

The holidays lend themselves to a bunch of humor. I think if you put your mind to it, you can find something funny about any special day.

10 Other Holidays This Weekend Besides Rosh Hashanah

10. For annoying right-wing radio personalities: Rush Hashanah
9. For 50's rock and roll bands: Rosh Hashanana
8. For exterminators: Roach Hashanah
7. For Jerry Seinfeld: Rosh Shoshana
6. For Iranians: Rosh Ha Shah
5. For Slam Dancers: Mosh Hashanah
4. If you're going to Zern's tonight: Don't Washashana
3. For Children's clothing: Oshkosh B' Goshashana
2. For Al's Diamond Cabaret: Tush Hashanah
1. For those who have slept with Madonna: Rash Hashanah

10 Dangerous Christmas Toys Gifts

10. Kenner Easy Bake Nuclear Power Plant
9. The Cabbage Patch Crack Pipe
8. Teddy Kennedy Ruxpin
7. G.I. Jeffrey Dahmer
6. Teenage Mutant Ninja Razor Blades
5. The Barbie '73 Pinto®
4. Mr. Hand Grenade Head
3. The Barbed Wire Slinky®
2. The Rockem Sockem Broken Condom
1. The Pee-Wee Herman Doll With The Kung-Fu Grip

10 Russian Christmas Traditions

10. Big man dressed in red creeps down chimney. Santa Claus follows.
9. Mistlestoli.
8. TASS reports strange sleigh like object spotted on radar. MiG-23 shoots it down.
7. Breadnog.
6. Jolly Old St. Nikolai.
5. Write letters to Santa. Request toilet paper.
4. Huddle by smoldering fire in weather beaten hovel hoping the KGB doesn't barge in and arrest you for not starving last week.
3. Wondering why you're not supposed to hate the Americans anymore.
2. Gather around the Christmas shrub and thank God for ridding Mother Russia of Hitler and Yakov Smirnoff.
1. Listening to hear if The Stalingrad School District is closed!

Comic Jim Kline grabbing my crotch, me grabbing my crotch, Phil grabbing no one's crotch, Raymond chust happy to be there.

10 Reindeer Names If Called By Michael Jackson

10. On Billy!
9. On Tommy!
8. On Stevie!
7. On Fire!
6. On Bobby!
5. On Chad!
4. On Amphetamines!
3. On Bubbles!
2. On Pokey!
1. On Estrogen!

10 Names Not Chosen For Bethlehem

10. Allentown
9. J.C. Ville
8. Manger-In-Hand
7. Stigmatanoy City
6. Thorndale
5. King of Kingston
4. Myrrhtztown
3. Christmas Village
2. Virginville
1. Walk On Watertown

10 Ways To Know You've Had A Little Too Much On St. Patrick's Day

10. You wake up today, and you've already had too much.
9. You dream you are standing naked in the street, and you wake up to find yourself standing naked in the street.
8. Your complexion is a nice shade of Kelly.

7. They deliver your mail to the barstool.
6. The cooked cabbage starts to smell good.
5. Teddy Kennedy says you've had enough.
4. You wake up and find yourself walking through K-Mart wearing a g-string and a goat mask.
3. You're riding in the back of the paddy wagon with a duck, two sheep and a big jar of mint jelly.
2. "Misten here, lister!"
1. At 7:00 tonight you're already telling someone, "You're the best friend I ever had."

10 Bad Valentine Poems

10. Roses are red. Violets are blue. I'm marrying Bob.
9. Roses are red. Grown by a farmer. Come over for dinner. Signed, Jeffrey Dahmer.
8. Roses are red. How about that? Sorry to say...I ran over your cat.
7. Roses are red. I hope that it snows. So I can then say that Antietam is closed.
6. Roses are reds. Violets are blues. I hope you like them. I got them for yous.
5. Roses are red. Let's go on a date. But first let's listen to a winter weather update.
4. Roses are red. They need some water. Sorry I'm late. I was banging your daughter.
3. Roses are red. I got you none. 'Cause on our last date I didn't get some.
2. Roses are red. This poem is garbled. It won't make the paper 'cause it ain't about marbles.
1. Roses are red. I want to have kids. So when I get home, it's "Whoomp, there it is!"

10 More Bad Valentine Poems

10. Roses are red. Wouldn't you say? Be careful if your Valentine's name is O.J.
9. Roses are red. Valentine Day ain't on Sundy. I hope your sweetheart isn't Ted Bundy.
8. Roses are red, and so's the rash you gave me.
7. Roses are red. Tulips are too. I'll meet you tomorrow up at the Penn View.
6. Roses are red. My thoughts I'm collecting. So glad to hear that you're not expecting.
5. Roses are red. Coal is black. Hope you're not going anywhere on Amtrak.
4. Roses are red. Sorry I haven't been home. I'll be back in town when you're done with premenstrual syndrome.
3. Roses are red. What do you want? Knock-knock. Who's there? Oh no! It's John DuPont!
2. Roses are red. Corny and phooey. So I got you a romantic getaway to the boro of Shoey!
1. Roses are red. Sorry I'm locked up. I sent you some flowers 'cause I heard you were knocked up.

Halloween is one of my favorite holidays. I love doing scary things like spelunking in Centralia, going to family reunions in West Virginia or having the doctor say, "I'm sorry, sir, that thermometer doesn't go in your mouth."

10 Other Scary Holidays Besides Halloween

10. For Asthmatics: Halloweeze
9. For Boy Scouts: Hallowebelo
8. For Eagles Lineman Bernard Williams after he got busted for pot: Halloweed

7. For Psychics: Halloweejee
6. For Sandy Duncan: Hallowheatthins
5. For Potty Trainers: Hallowee-wee
4. For Drunks: Ernest and Julio Galloween
3. For USA For Africa: Hallowee are the world...Wee are the people....
2. For Champions: Hallowheaties
1. For People who wobble, but they don't fall down: Halloweebles

10 Halloween Candies That Never Made It

10. Chocolate, nuggat and rodent: Three Mousekateers Bar
9. Candy coated doggie-doo: B & M's
8. Chocolate, caramel, nuts and old Nikes: Sneakers Bar
7. Chocolate, peanut butter and jockstraps: Pee-Wee Reese's Cup
6. Chocolate, caramel, nuggat and cats: Milky Spay
5. Chewy chocolate in the shape of toes: Footsie Rolls
4. Chocolate, wafer and litter box: Kit Krap Bar
3. Chocolate, peanuts and proctologists: Butter Finger
2. Chocolate, raisins and that little bag Mike had when he flew with the Blue Angels: Chunky
1. Chocolate covered breasts: Boobers

Political Stuff

"Dave Stein? It is so good to finally meet you! I just love Kutztown. Say, who's the chick next to you?"

I wish I had a dollar for every person who asked me how I come up with this stuff. I don't know. It just happens. I'm the kind of person who sits around wondering if The Pope thinks to himself, "Man, I'm The Pope!" I was watching the L.A. riots thinking that bashing a man's head in during your TV debut is no way to get to Hollywood. You need an agent. I was also thinking that The Phillies could have used a couple of those LAPD sluggers.

Do you think prisons should run specials on executions? "It's a sizzling Summer of savings! Come on down, we're having a cell-a-bration sale! Fry one get one free!"

For first few years of The Mike and Dave Show we had a ton of fun with the local elected officials in Reading and Berks. It was hard to believe that some of these morons were directing *and* creating policy. We poked fun at them. If a councilman or a school board member said something or did something stupid, we talked about it. If an elected official was charged with a crime, we

No one was going to mess with Bill that day. Would you?

talked about it. Unfortunately, since no one had ever done this on Reading radio in the past, it was a shock to both the station and the elected officials. It turns out that the people we were discussing on the air were a bunch of thin-skinned pussies who, if they were elected officials in New York or L.A. or any slightly more progressive area would have been laughed out of town!

However, this is Berks County. They would call the station and complain to management about Mike and Dave. Guess who got in trouble? The owners of the station didn't care if a school board member or a commissioner was an asshole, all they cared about was that their "busy" day was interrupted with a phone call from an elected official.

I have chosen to not make this a "tell-all book." I just want to have fun and make a few folks smile. In this category of "political lists" don't expect to see the names of infamous controversial local officials.

One of Berks County's true gems, State Senator Mike O'Pake, Mike and Dave at the State Capitol Building after we rode bikes to Harrisburg protesting the screwing of Berks County by Governor Ridge.

Enjoy some of the more political 7:20 Lists:

10 Differences Between O.J. and Hillary

10. He's been acquitted.
9. One looks like they could still play football. The other just spent a year and a half in jail.
8. Paula Jones is still alive.
7. White Ford Bronco...White Water....
6. She's the First Lady. He can't remember his first lady.
5. O.J.'s only been screwed by the President on his tax return.
4. Sometimes it's her *words* that cut like a knife.
3. Both have daughters who are wondering how their fathers will make a living in 1997.
2. (the next 2 are really rude:) The President would love a Heisman Trophy and a dead wife.
1. Both have spouses who don't inhale.

10 Expressions the Clintons Use For Doing The Nasty

10. Campaign Stumpin'.
9. Working in the Oval Office.
8. Goin' down to Arkansas.
7. Taking a Harris Poll.
6. Stroking a special interest group.
5. Screwing the taxpayers.
4. Flappin' the East Wing.
3. Firing up Air Force One.
2. Hoppin' on The Joint Chiefs of Staff.
1. Pushing a Bill through Congress.

10 Things Dan Quayle Hated About George Bush

10. Always called him "Scooter."
9. Grounded him once for calling Monaco and asking for Prince Albert In A Can.
8. Never warned him Murphy Brown was a fictional character.
7. Took away his "see and spell."
6. Would never tell him how the Oval Office got its name.
5. Never let *him* bomb anyone.
4. Wouldn't return his calls.
3. Yelled at him for making bubbles in White House Pool.
2. Made him study on Saturday nights.
1. He lived.

After Denny's was sued for racial discrimination. We came up with this list. With the way some people think, it's hard to believe it's almost the turn of the century.

Former Governor Bob Casey and I talking on the air about how much he loves The Mike and Dave Show.

10 Items On The New Denny's Menu

10. Ham on White.
9. The Lynch...er...Lunch Special.
8. Grand Dragon Breakfast.
7. Hot Burning Cross Buns.
6. Vanilla Milk Shakes.
5. The Marge Schott Burger.
4. 2 Eggs and a side of Racist Toast.
3. Fresh Squeezed Orange Noose.
2. L.A. Police Club Sandwich.
1. The Grand Klan Breakfast.

MEMORANDUM

TO: David Stein
cc: Ragan Henry; Mike Shannon; Stein File
FROM: Don Kidwell
DATE: November 28, 1994
RE: Recent Moron Of The Week

* *

Please be informed that any future complaints of this nature will result in a minimum suspension of 1 week, without pay. You must discontinue the practice of ready! Shoot! AIM! Mike Shannon assures me the moron of the week feature has been discontinued.

Excerpt from confidential memo in my file.

Movies in the Theater As We Speak

Whenever I couldn't come up with a 7:20 List, I could always resort to the category called, "Movies In The Theater As We Speak." I would just go to the entertainment section of whatever fish-wrap I bought that morning and do a little play-on-words with the movie titles.

10 Movies In The Theater As We Speak

10. Harrison Ford in the Tom Clancy Christmas Thriller, *Clear and Present Manger.*
9. Disney mates a cat and a gorilla in *The Lion Kong.*
8. The story of a body guard for the cast of Entertainment Tonight, *Guarding Tesh.*
7. Clint Eastwood as O.J. Simpson in *White Ford Bronco Billy.*
6. Dustin Hoffman as a savant Dutchman in *Rainman The Amish Comic.*
5. Steven Segal in the violent sequel to the classic Katherine Hepburn/Henry Fonda film, *On Deadly Pond.*
4. Elvis with stomach troubles, *Upper G.I. Blues.*
3. William Kennedy Smith and his uncle in *Bill and Ted's Excellent Adventure.*
2. A Far East family watches your car in, *Get The Joy Luck Club.*
1. Steven Spielberg's epic film set in gay Germany, *Shindler's Lisp.*

10 More Movies In The Theater As We Speak

10. Macauly Culkin as a little leaguer who forgets his cup, *The Nutcracker.*
9. Jack Nicholson as the guy trying to unionize prostitutes, *Boffa.*
8. Dinosaurs invade Al's Diamond Cabaret, *Niceassic Park.*

7. Harrison Ford stars as a bald cartoon character without a mouth, *Regarding Henry*.
6. Daniel Day Lewis stars as a duck in *My Webbed Foot*.
5. Sharon Stone as a bisexual computer geek in *Basic and FORTRAN Instinct*.
3. They find out the real story of the 76ers in *The Truth About Katz and Dogs*.
2. Andie McDowell in a Pennsylvania Dutch Romantic Comedy, *Four Weddings and a Funnel Cake*.
1. Leslie Nielson as an ostracized Amishman in *The Naked Shun*.

Yes, I am wearing something under that grass skirt!

10 More Movies In The Theater As We Speak

10. Cher stars in *The Hand That Robs The Cradle.*
9. A dyslexic criminal commits crimes of sin in *NEVES.*
8. Strippers in New Holland...*4-H Showgirls.*
7. Those creepy, kooky Iraqis in *The Saddams Family.*
6. Walt Disney dives into female problems, *Beauty and the Yeast.*
5. Bette Midler and James Caan entertain a bunch of gentiles in *For The Goys.*
4. Arnold Schwarzeneggar as a gigolo in *The Sperminator.*
3. The Potter County Story, *I Married My Cousin Vinnie.*
2. President Clinton in *Waiting To Inhale.*
1. O.J. Simpson in *Cutthroat Island.*

10 More Movies In The Theater As We Speak

10. Greek mythological figure Prometheus starring in *Homeward Unbound.* (sorry, that's clever.)
9. Fast food in Korea repeats itself in *Ground Dog Day.*
8. The Christmas horror film...*Young Frankincense.*
7. Old member of the morning show in his first martial arts movie...*Morty Combat.*
6. A Movie about Spanish cooking in space...*A Pollo 13.*
5. Mr. and Mrs. Chamberlain star in *How To Make An American Wilt.*
4. The Amish horror flick, *Rosemary's Buggy.*
3. James Bond fights for what is right in the 6th Congressional District, *Holdeneye.*
2. Chinese Hockey Players...*Mighty Tasty Ducks*!
1. Classic Woody Allen Movie, *Play It Again, Soon-Yi.*

Y-102 and Mike & Dave

This may look like the Presidential limo, but it's actually the car they send for us each morning. That's Mike puking in the back seat.

The medium we have on The Mike and Dave Show is a powerful one. I personally feel that self-effacing humor is the best. I especially like "self-effacing" humor when someone else is the butt of the joke. We're always complaining about the way the station treats us. It's discouraging when we don't get a raise because the station budget was blown on a double-remote broadcast at the Giant. So, quite often, we poke fun at Y-102 and Mike and Dave.

It was a sad day in my life when Mike decided to hang up his headphones and take a gig over at Maple Grove Raceway. I think I speak for all of our listeners when I say, "HALLELULAH!!!! HE'S BACK!" You know, of course, the reason he came back was his disillusioning realization that drag racing was not fast guys in dresses.

The infamous Y-102 Pepsi Super Roving Radio. God, we hated that thing.

A lot has changed since 1988. Here are 10 differences between The Mike and Dave Show then and The Mike and Dave Show now:

10 Differences Between The Mike and Dave Show, then and now

10. Mike still laughs at Dave's jokes, but he gets most of them now.
9. Their wives are allowed in bars now.
8. Now a big party night is staying up to watch Frazier.
7. Chicks still come up to us all the time, but now they want to know if we know Freddie. *
6. Morning off-air conversation includes, "How's your back and did you move your bowels."
5. We pee a lot more now.
4. Mike has done daring stuff like drag racing and flying with the Blue Angels. Dave has walked through the Buttonwood Street IGA at night!
3. The music we play doesn't suck anymore.
2. When we started, George Burns was a kid.
1. Now that the station has made tens of millions of dollars off The Mike and Dave Show, they only give us grief and make us feel worthless twice a year instead of the normal 5 or 6.

Freddie Isettie, our friend and co-worker.

10 Ways To Know Mike Is Getting Old

10. Recently started calling wife, "Mommy."
9. Buying a lottery ticket benefits him.
8. Daily complaints about the fresh price of produce.
7. Thinking of trading his mini-van in for something less sporty.

6. Starts every sentence with, "When I was your age..."
5. Goes to Al's for the food.
4. Can't remember topic of today's 7:20 List.
3. Gets decent buzz off Metamucil.
2. AARP application on his desk.
1. Knows where it is. Knows what it is. Can't remember where to put it.

And in regard to equal time:

10 Ways To Know Dave Is Getting Old

10. Chicks in bars refer to him as, "Mr. Stein."
9. Thought David Cassidy was cool the first time he came along.
8. Rogaine, Rogaine, Rogaine.
7. Seriously thinking about coaching T-Ball.
6. Still believes there was some tangible message in the Pink Floyd songs; when if fact, it's just that they were stoned when they wrote them.
5. Afternoon trip to men's room steadily increasing on list of "fun things to do."
4. Recently caught sporting the open-toed sandal and dress socks look.
3. Sits in barber shop with a bunch of other guys just bitching about stuff.
2. Doesn't find much humor in the "I've fallen, and I can't get up Lady" anymore.
1. Still thinks crack is a good piece of ass.

In case you just got off the BARTA bus, or you've just fallen off the scrapple truck, Mike Browne flew with The U.S. Navy Blue Angel Flight Demonstration Team in August of 1995.

Clearly, this was a highlight of his life, but for me, it was an endless source of morning show material.

10 Reasons The Blue Angels Might Reject Mike For His Flight

10. Flight suit doesn't come in Spandex®.
9. Navy is already at budget on military barf bags.
8. Mike's fondness for ordering-out over cockpit microphone.
7. Would not allow Mike to sing "In The Navy" during flight.
6. They remember the time when Mike called Admiral Hadly, "Spanky."
5. The Richard I. Hart Insurance Agency of Mount Penn won't insure the F/A-18 Hornet.
4. Don't ask. Don't tell.
3. Mike's reputation makes Tailhook look like Catholic School.
2. Doesn't know how to fly.
1. Blood alcohol level too low to be in line with The Blues.

Me and "Ole #7". That's Mike puking in the back seat.

For a while, I was calling Mike, "Tom" for Tom Cruise. When you think about it, they do have a lot in common. Tom's been in Cocktail. Mike's had a few cocktails in him. Tom has played a vampire. Mike has some nasty incisors. Tom played in Rainman. Mike is an excellent driver.

10 Reasons Mike Deserves To Be Commander Of The Blue Angels

10. What? With the 45 minutes of flight time he has logged? You kidding me?
9. It would be so cool!
8. No chance of being president of the NHRA.
7. Danger? He's driven the Starcruiser *and* the Giant Music Radio!
6. Blue Angel Flight Surgeon hands out free condoms and Tylenol.
5. Blues tired of that "V" look for their pilots.

Comedians Jim Carrol, Jim Kline and The Blue Angels after a show at The Reading Comedy Outlet. (The Blues had 12 pitchers of beer and many shots...AND flew the next day!)

4. Blue Angels are not allowed to go to strip joints and neither is Mike.
3. Seems easily adaptable to military life.
2. Heard Tommy Frank needs a radio job again.
1. First ever F/A-18 Mini-Van.

In the past 8 years Mike has had 2 discs removed from his back and double-hernia surgery. I have had a major league broken arm, and Sevé has had a head tumor, his claws removed and his balls cut off. Luckily, none of our doctors confused us with Seve'.

We called Mike in the operating room just before his hernia surgery. His doctor wouldn't let us broadcast the operation live. I did the next best thing.

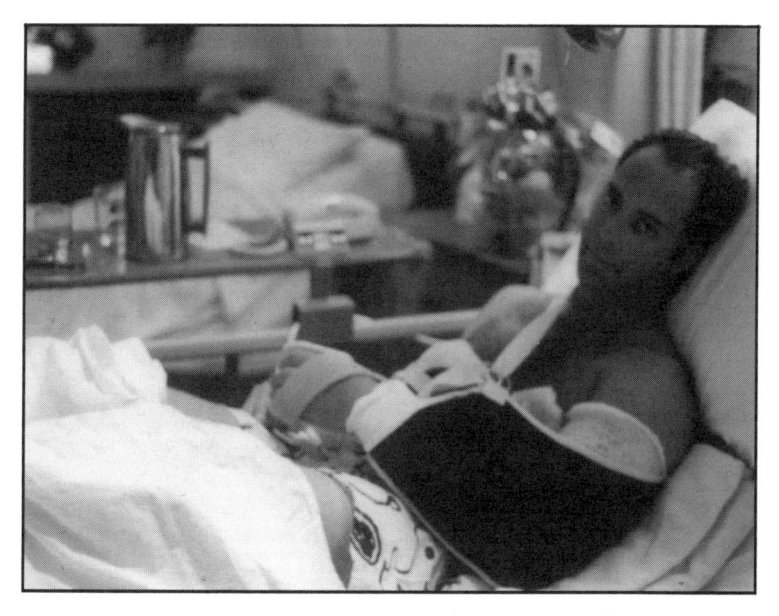

Don't try to play baseball at the age of 28 after a five-year layoff. OUCH! (note the Snoopy underwear!)

10 Things Overheard During Mike's Hernia Surgery

10. "While I'm down there do you want to be Jewish?"
9. "Hey, where's Dave?"
8. "Giggle, giggle, giggle."
7. "You may feel a little pressure."
6. "Hey, Mike. Joe Dell is on the line."
5. "Dr. Bobbitt! Calling Dr. Bobbitt!"
4. "Ooh, it must be cold in here."
3. "Is it safe?"
2. "Whoops."
1. "Wait a minute! I thought you said I was going to Alvernia!"

No question about it. Winter in Berks County sucks! If Mike and Dave could work anywhere in the world, I think we'd still hate Winter. Simply because our bad Berks Winter experiences would follow us everywhere.

10 Things Heard On The Mike and Dave Show If They Spent Winter In Hawaii

10. "This tanning index update is brought to you by The King Kamehameha City Family Restaurant."
9. "The Waikiki Beach busses 1, 2, 3 and 4 are operating for surfboard riders only."
8. "The Molokai School District is closed due to lava flow."
7. "Thanks to the folks at Take 2 Poi in the Hilo Road Plaza for supplying breakfast today."
6. "The luau at the Oahu Senior Center has been postponed due to a slight breeze out of the West."
5. "Anyone with a 4-wheel drive vehicle that can take a tourist to Jack Lords house call…"

4. "Man, this sun sure sucks, Dave." "You got that right, Mike!"
3. "The Governor has declared a state of emergency. There's a cloud."
2. "The Little Grass Skirt Nursery School of The Big Island is open for day care only."
1. "Check this out, Brah. I'm not making this up. Just got this over the wire. In a place called Reading, Pennsylvania, people shovel out parking spaces and then they put lawn chairs in them. Can you believe that! That's right! It's time for Moron of the Week!"

What if we did a morning show in the Far East?

10 Things Heard On The Mike and Dave Show in the Far East

10. "We've got a wintry mix of volcano, earthquake and monsoon…however, all parochial schools are open."
9. "We'd like to thank the folks at Take 2 Dog for supplying the breakfast today."
8. "You're tuned to a clearly more superior sound system than anything manufactured by those lazy Westerners."
7. "Coming up…this week's #1 for the 8th week in a row! David Hasselhoff!"
6. "Coors Light and Radio Free Beijing give you a chance to go to the World Ping Pong Championships!"
5. "There's a tie up on the Ho Chi Minh today…in evidence at the ox crossing."
4. "Hey, Mikey-San…What do you call cookies in the Philippines? Manila Wafers! Get it? Manila!"

3. "Broadcasting from high atop the big outlet monument on Mt. Fuji."
2. "Mike, I gotta tell ya. That program director, Al? He's so Hanoiing!"
1. "Here's some ZZ Top...Mao, Mao, Mao...."

If we are still doing the morning show in the year 2013, it will be our 25th anniversary. We'd still be #1 because Y-102 will still be the only radio station you can pick up at work!

10 Things About The Mike and Dave Show in The Year 2013

10. The 7:20 List will be brought to you by Depends.
9. The show will start at 4:00AM because we can't sleep any longer than that.
8. More commercials so we can pee.
7. Morty will be dead.
6. We'll have a brand spankin' new cat!
5. Mike will be broadcasting from a Craftmatic Adjustable Bed.
4. When we sound cranky, it won't be a "bit."
3. Station collectibles include the Y-102 Enema Bag
2. California Bar and Grill hosts morning show anniversary with "All You Can Eat Oatmeal."
1. I'll still be writing the 7:20 List at 7:10.

This Stuff is Just Plain Funny!

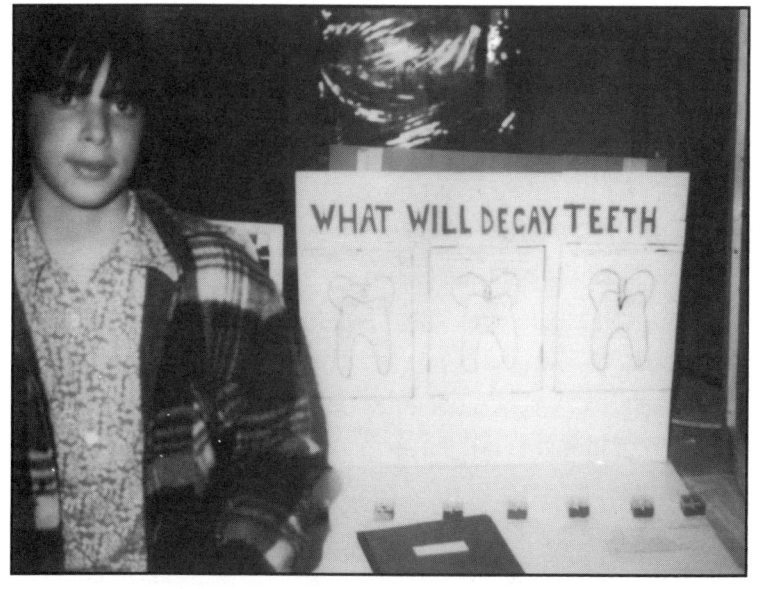

No kidding, this was my 7th grade science fair project down at Perk Valley. Little did I know I would move to Berks County later in life!

Some of the best 7:20 Lists don't fall into a category. They are just darn funny. For example, one list asked if Mao Tsetung was Chinese for oral sex. Another claimed Michael Jackson returned home from a trip to England when he found out Big Ben was a clock. Yet another said O.J. went to Great Britain after the trial because he thought it was *Rockingham Palace*.

10 Misconceptions About Poetry

10. "Iambic Pentameter" is not an Olympic sport.
9. No one ever asked "Where's Ralph Waldo Emerson?"
8. Walt Whitman was not named after a bridge.
7. Longfellow was not Clarence Thomas' favorite poet.
6. Poe is not the opposite of rich.
5. Robert Frost did not write, "Two roads diverge in a snowy woods," about 183 North and The Road To Nowhere.
4. Joyce Carol Oates is not a new breakfast cereal.
3. e.e. cummings is not the sound a chimp makes when having sex.
2. A B B A is not a singing group.
1. An example of fine poetry does not start out: "There once was a girl with angina…"

10 Types of Snow

10. The Mitch Williams Snow...It missed us.
9. The Michael Jackson Snow...All the elementary schools are closed.
8. The Urologist Snow...It's yellow.
7. The Madonna Snow...It's laying.
6. The Linda Lovelace Snow...It's deep.
5. The Darryl Strawberry Snow...Just a dusting.
4. Jack Kevorkian Snow...You don't have to worry about the roads.
3. The Eunich Snow...No snowballs.
2. The Three Mile Island Snow...4 feet.
1. The O.J. Snow...Who cares. We're sick of it.

10 Reasons To Put Out On Prom Night*

10. Looking for any excuse to take off that wrist corsage.
9. He <u>did</u> buy dinner.
8. You want him to call again, don't ya?
7. Let's see...your Mom and Dad are both 36...it's kinda like tradition, right?
6. Guilts him into signing yearbook.
5. Ensure graduation award, "Most Likely To Conceive."
4. Comforting to know you've blown something other than just $200 on a dress.
3. "Morning after" regrets help you better prepare for life.
2. Prom night pregnancies increase "Knights in White Satin" royalties.
1. Helps you get invited again.

*Please, no phone calls. This is funny.

10 Things If The Mob Took Over The Health Care Industry

10. It's not loan sharking, it's a "co-pay."
9. It's not protection money, it's a premium."
8. "Dis policy does not cover small holes in the back of the head, or if a small accident should befall you."
7. "I'd like you to meet Dr. Jimmy 'The Knife' Cusmino. He specializes in thoracic surgery."
6. Welcome to St. Joseph Hospital, Hotel and Casino.
5. The nurse will give you something to make you sleep better...with the fishes.
4. The Federal Patient Protection Program.
3. "Before we put you into this meat grinder, would you mind filling out these forms?"
2. "I'm sorry, Dr. Hoffa's been transferred to a long-term care facility."
1. "I'm gonna give you an enema bag you can't refuse."

10 Euphemisms For Having a Bad Hair Day

10. Struck by The Ugly Comb.
9. Celebrating Don King Day.
8. Einsteined.
7. Rentin' a Movie Tonight.
6. Something Has Happened in the Motorcade!
5. Jerry Lewis Curl.
4. Babushka'd
3. Dippity-Doo-Daahed.
2. Cy Sperlingitis.
1. Bad Head.

Wife in Va. severs man's penis; surgeons restore it

By Marylou Tousignant and Carlos Sanchez
WASHINGTON POST

MANASSAS, Va. — A 26-year-old suburban Washington man whose wife cut off his penis with a kitchen knife while he slept yesterday morning was reported in satisfactory condition last night after 9½ hours of surgery to reattach the organ, officials said.

Authorities learned of the incident when the man showed up at a local hospital about 5 a.m. Police officers were dispatched to his nearby apartment to search for the missing penis, but could not find it.

About the same time, the man's wife called authorities from a pay phone to say she had been raped, had fled the apartment "in a panic," unknowingly taking the penis with her, and had thrown the penis out the window of her car at an intersection near the city line of Manassas Park, Va.

The penis was recovered at the intersection, packed in ice and taken by fire and rescue personnel to Prince William Hospital in Manassas, where the surgical reattachment began shortly after 6 a.m., said James T. Sehn, a urologist who was one of two doctors who participated in the delicate operation.

Prosecutor Paul B. Ebert said last night that the couple, who were not identified, "had been experiencing considerable domestic difficulty."

"Her bags were packed," Ebert said of the 24-year-old wife.

The woman told police that her husband raped her shortly before she cut off two-thirds of his penis.

"After he went to sleep, she got a kitchen knife," Ebert said.

A police spokesman said the woman was released after being treated as a rape victim at the same hospital where her husband was undergoing surgery.

Police charged the woman last night with aggravated malicious wounding, a felony that carries a maximum penalty of 40 years in jail. Ebert said police had been unable to interview the man, and that no charges had been brought in connection with the woman's rape allegation.

Former neighbors of the couple said the woman often complained of being beaten by her husband.

"He was just a kid, and she was caught in a terrible, terrible situation," said a man who asked not to be identified.

"She obviously needed help," said another neighbor. The couple reportedly separated at least once, in October 1991.

Penile reattachments, although not medically difficult, are rare.

"It's safe to say that fewer than 100 have ever been done," said Charles B. Cuono, a professor of surgery at Yale University School of Medicine, who could recall only three such surgeries there in 12 years.

The infamous newspaper article with my notes and highlights marked in pencil.

10 Movies To Be Made About Lorena Bobbitt

10. Little Chop of Horrors.
9. The Ted Turner Civil War Epic: Got-his-bird.
8. Bob & Carol & Ted & Penis.
7. The Incredible Shrinking Man.
6. The Redford Western: Where's-a-my-a Johnson?
5. It's a Wonderful Knife.
4. Slice Castles.
3. Maybe Dick.
2. Castrateblanca.
1. Presumed Impotent.

10 Things John Bobbitt Said On The Way Out Of The Courthouse

10. "I do have a soft spot for her."
9. "I hate to cut you off, but I gotta go."
8. "Justice has been severed."
7. "Velcro, velcro, velcro!"
6. "Ecstatic? I'm in stitches!"
5. "I'm trying to keep a stiff upper lip."
4. "Maybe I'm pregnant, but I've got a craving for sliced pickles."
3. "Endorsements? I'm mulling over offers from Wang and John Henry."
2. "Wanna see my scar?"
1. "I've got to tie up some loose ends."

10 Things At Upscale Turkey Hills (or any convenience stores)

10. The Twinkie Cart.
9. The Slurpee Steward.
8. They ask you, "And how would you like your burrito microwaved?"
7. You need reservations to rob it.
6. The Slim Jims don't have prices on them.
5. They have stoned and not stoned sections.
4. Valet loitering.
3. The cops are dressed better.
2. No jacket, no tie, no service.
1. Only 2 students allowed in at one time…3 if they're Ivy League.

10 New Postal Slogans

10. We're not all armed.
9. We'll lick it for you.
8. We deliver as fast as we reload.
7. Duck.
6. Stamps. It's brain food.
5. Whaddya want for 32¢?
4. We won't mace your dog too bad.
3. Mail fever…Catch it!
2. Rat-a-tat-tat.
1. Neither rain, nor sleet, nor hail of bullets…

Many times, the list is only good in the spoken form. It may be the way I accent a word, or perhaps I change my voice. The following list is one of my favorites, but you have to use your imagination.

10 Things You Say To People When You Have No Idea What Their Name Is

10. Yo, Bud!
9. Heeeey…How ya doin'?
8. Big Guuuuy!
7. Hey, Chief!
6. We were just talking about yoooou.
5. They let anybody in here.
4. Well look who it is!
3. My Man!
2. Duuuuude!
1. There he is!

Thanks for taking this picture, Mom. David Stein, circa 2023 AD.

I've mentioned how many lists start out as a crazy idea and come to fruition on the back of a cocktail napkin at The Firehouse Bar & Restaurant or CB & G. One night Mrs. Stein and I had just attended the ritual circumcision of an eight day old Jewish male, a briss. We then caught up with some friends who had already had a few bottles of cabernet. We came up with the following list. Check out the wine and food-stained doily from the table that night.

10 Things You Shouldn't Do at a Briss
10. Serve pigs in a blanket.
9. Ask The Moyel if he left a tip.
8. Yell, "Oops!"
7. Use the Ginsu.
6. Let Muhammad Ali perform the cutting.
5. Wonder what's in scrapple, anyway.
4. Yell, "Off with 'is 'ead!"
3. Contrary to popular belief, should not be performed in the back of a Mercury Marquis.
2. Ask the question, "You gonna eat that?"
1. Show off yours.

10 BRIS FAUX PAS

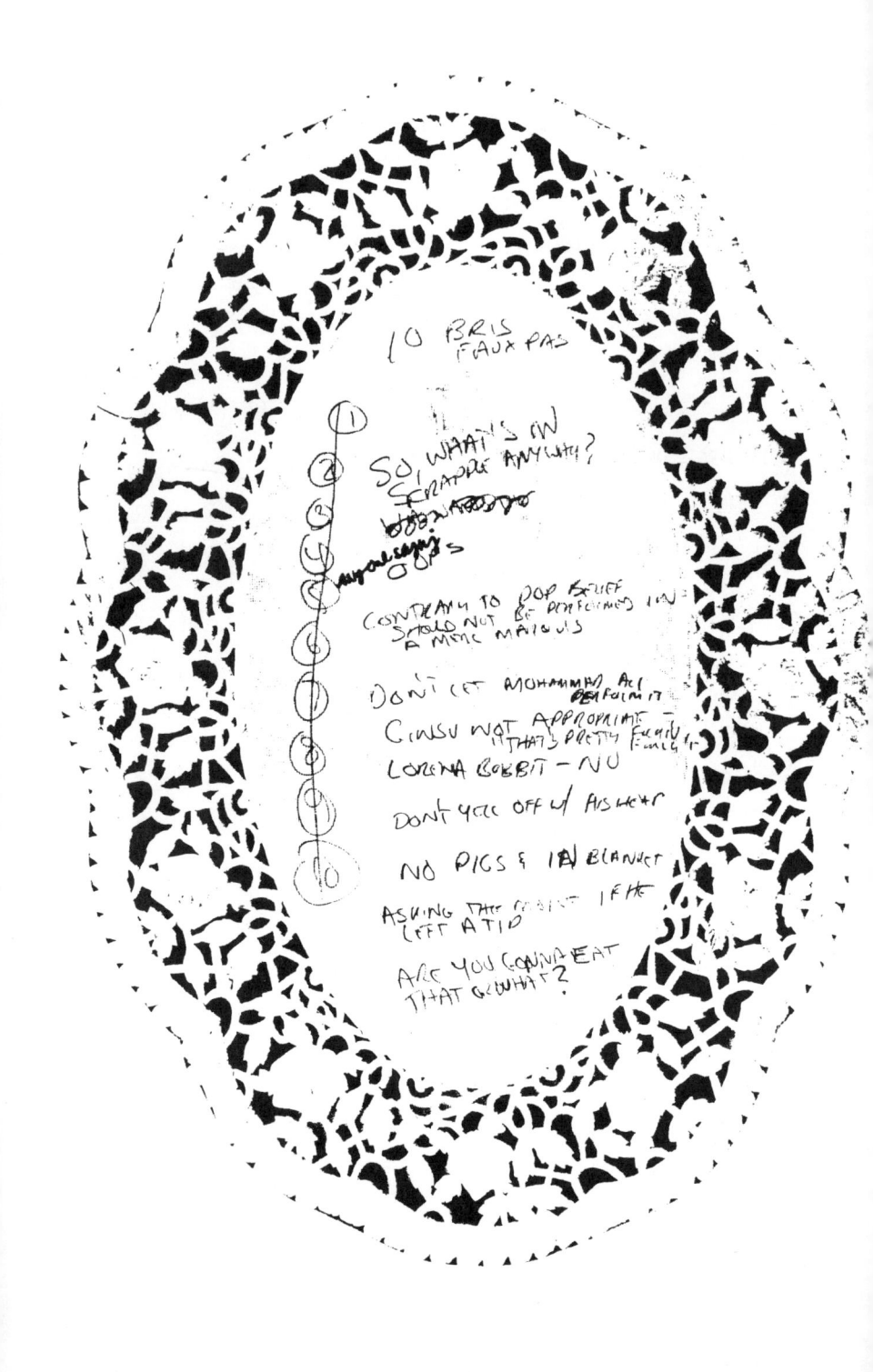

1. SO, WHAT'S IN SCRAPPLE ANYWAY?
2.
3.
4. OOPS
5. CONTRARY TO POP BELIEF, SHOULD NOT BE PERFORMED IN A MIME MARQUIS
6. DON'T LET MOHAMMED ALI PERFORM IT
7. CIRCUMSION NOT APPROPRIATE - THAT'S PRETTY FUNNY
8. LORENA BOBBIT - NO
9. DON'T YOU OFF W/ HIS WEAR
10. NO PIGS & IN BLANKET

ASKING THE RABBI IF HE LEFT A TIP

ARE YOU GONNA EAT THAT G(W)HAT?

Plays on Words

Nice 30th birthday present. Looks like she could kick my ass!

No question, one of our most popular 7:20 Lists is when we have a little fun with words. The following are my favorite "play on words" lists:

10 Other Ways To Leave Your Lover
(As In The Paul Simon Song)

10. Kick Her Outa Bed, Fred.
9. Give Her The Cooties, Hootie.
8. Say, "See You Lato, Kato!"
7. Ask Her For A Menage A Trois, Francois
6. Tell Her You're Someone Else, Sybil.
5. Take Him To Dr. Kevorkian's Place, Grace.
4. Spin Your Head Around And Damn Him To Eternal Hell, Michelle.
3. Just Leave That Ho, Joe.
2. Change Your Sex, Rex.
1. Tell Her They Cut You Loose, Juice!

10 Other Invasions Besides D-Day

10. Invasion Of Franklin St....V.D. Day
9. Invasion Of Kids At The Shores Of New Jersey...Fake I.D. Day
8. Invasion Of Dead Rock Stars...O.D. Day
7. Invasion Of The Sticks Of Berks County...R.D. Day
6. Invasion Of Churches In The Afternoon...C.C.D. Day
5. Invasion Of Clark Gable's House...Judy, Judy, Judy Day
4. Invasion Of The Geriatric Center...Oldee Day
3. Invasion Of The Pasta Aisle At The Giant...Chef Boy-Ar-Dee Day

2. Invasion Of Story Book Characters...Tweedle Dum And Tweedle Dee Day
1. Invasion Of Camptown...All The Doo Dah Day!

10 Latin Phrases And Their Meanings

10. Et Tu Brute ...(Where's The Beef?)
9. E. Pluribus Unum...(I'm Not Gonna Pay A Lot For This Muffler)
8. A Maxima, Ad Minuma...(Tastes Great, Less Filling)
7. In Absentia...(He's A Congressman)
6. Semper Fidelis...(Don't Mess With The Marines)
5. Post Hoc, Ergo Propter Hoc...(Does This Mean We Have To Get Married?
4. Meum Et Tuum...(He Goes Both Ways)
3. Dum Spiro Spero...(That's The Vice-President)
2. Veni, Vidi, Vici...(Lather, Rinse, Repeat)
1. Esse Quam Videri...(I'll Show You Mine If You Show Me Yours)

10 Other Work Out Slogans Besides "No Pain/No Gain"

10. Working Out To Channel 69 News...No Pain/No Kathy Craine
9. Working Out On SEPTA...No Pain/No Train
8. Working Out With The Reincarnated...No Pain/No Shirley MacClaine
7. Working Out With John Dupont...No Pain/You're Insane
6. Working Out With Professor Higgins...No Pain/ No Rain In Spain Falls Mainly On The Plain
5. Working Out With Old Time Baseball Players...No Pain/No Spahn And Sain And Two Days Of Rain (Funny If You're A Baseball Fan)

4. Working Out On Fantasy Island-No Pain/No Plane
3. Working Out With A Fat Drug Addict...No Pain/No Vein
2. Working Out With A Sadist...No Pain/No Fun
1. Working Out With The Gay Tarzan...No Pain/No Jane!

10 Jewish Super Heroes (You Have To Say The Last Names With The Letters "M-A-N" Pronounced "Min")

10. Moishe Superman
9. Irv Batman
8. Speedy Gonzalez (Funny...Doesn't Look It.)
7. Captain Marvelwitz
6. Abe Aquaman
5. Seymour Ultraman
4. Heman...Rabbi Of The Universe
3. Sam Spiderman
2. Sandy Koufax
1. Jesus

10 Other Lingerie Stores Besides Victoria's Secret

10. For People With Sore Throats...Victoria Sucrets
9. For Cross Dressers...Victor/Victoria Secrets
8. For Employees Of Mel's Diner...Vic Taybec Secrets
7. For People Dismembered In Helicopter Accidents...Vic Morrow Secrets
6. For People With Chest Colds...Vicks Vapor Rub Secrets
5. For Your Boss...Victoria Secretaries
4. For Residents Of Japan...Victora-Tora-Tora Secrets
3. For The Psycho-Bitch Who Shoots Up Malls...Victoria Seegrist
2. For Horses...Victoria Secretariats
1. For The Social Diseased In Your Life...Victoria Secretions

Remember the quarterback for the Eagles, Bubby Brister? How much respect does a guy get in the huddle when his name is Bubby? Here are a couple of lists of people who would have lost a lot of respect had they been named Bubby:

10 people who would have lost a lot of respect had they been named Bubby

10. Pope Bubby The Sixth
9. Anchorman...Bubby Cronkite
8. Dictator...Bubby Bonaparte
7. Poet...Bubby Wadsworth Longfellow
6. Inventor...Bubby Graham Bell
5. Enterprise Captain...Bubby T. Kirk
4. Judge Bubby Ito
3. Civil Rights Leader...Bubby Luther King, Jr.
2. Soviet Leader...Bubby Breshnev
1. Famous Prophet...Bubby The Baptist

10 More Bubbies

10. World War II General...Bubby S. Patton
9. Sculptor...Bubby Da Vinci
8. Famous Brothers...John And Bubby Kennedy
7. Chinese Leader...Bubby Chow Ping
6. Royal Leader Of England...Queen Bubby
5. Famous Scary Guy...Bubby Kruger
4. Famous Savior...Bubby Christ
3. Famous Comedian...Bubby The Amish Comic
2. Rootenist Tootinest Varmint In The West...Bubby Sam
1. Famous Civil Rights Advocate...Bubby X

10 Famous Dicks

10. Dick Tracy
9. Dick Hertz
8. Dick Nixon
7. Dick York
6. Dick Cranium
5. Dick Sargent
4. Dick Thornburgh
3. Ridiculous
2. Fairliegh Dickinson
1. Tom Ridge

10 Famous Phillie Third Basemen Besides Michael Jack Schmidt

10. 3rd Sacker Turned Halloween Character…Michael Jack O' Lantern
9. 3rd Sacker Turned Tux Salesman…Michael Jack O' Reilly
8. 3rd Sacker Turned Fast Food Mogul…Michael Jack-In-The-Box
7. 3rd Sacker Turned Leader Of Iran…Michael Jack Shah
6. 3rd Sacker Turned Philadelphia Newscaster…Michael Jack Thomas-Laury
5. 3rd Sacker Turned Space Creature…Michael Jack 2 D 2
4. 3rd Sacker Turned Porn Star…Michael Jack Silver
3. 3rd Sacker Turned Rooster…Michael Jack Leghorn
2. 3rd Sacker Turned Scuba Diver…Michael Jack Cousteau
1. 3rd Sacker Turned Singer Formerly Known As Prince " ."

Bad Business Names

Gotta have a picture of Dad, if I have a picture of Mom.

If you open up a business, make sure it has a good name. Here Are Two Lists...

10 Bad Business Names

10. For a fast food chain: E. Coli King
9. For a physicians group: Vaseline And Rubber Glove Health Associates
8. The Betty Ford Pharmacy
7. Sleepy-Time Security Guards
6. Ed's Sewer, Drain And Sandwich Shop
5. Bob's Funeral Home And Comedy Club
4. For a print shop: Sam's Pronting
3. Family planning office: House Of Birth Control
2. For a shoe store: Bill's Plumbing
1. The Do-It-Yourself Sperm Bank

10 More Bad Business Names

10. The Really Cold Instrument Ob-Gyn Group
9. For a theme park: Hannibal Lectorland
8. For a fun food drinkery: P.J. Dingleberrys
7. For a speech therapist: She Sells Sea Shells Speech And Spit World
6. The Drop The Brat Off Here Pre-School
5. The Sucking Chest Wound Gun Shop
4. Ed's Abortion Warehouse
3. The Dahmer Diner
2. Near Miss Airlines
1. Jerky's Artificial Insemination

Fears and Phobias

My brother and I taking our last leaks before the wedding. Ain't that a pisser?
(not shown: the Rabbi and the Priest.)

So Many Folks Are Afraid Of Things. Here Are Some Of The More Lesser Known Phobias:

10 Fears And Phobias

10. Fear of Vic Taybec...Flobia.
9. Fear of Harry Kalas...What's The Scobia?
8. Fear of Ethel Merman...There's No Business Like Shobia.
7. Fear of The Pep Boys...Manny Mobia.
6. Fear of Oriental Architecture...Pagodaphobia.
5. Fear of Franklin Street...Hobia.
4. Fear of Not Getting Past First Base On A Date...Nobia.
3. Fear of L&B Dodge...Joebia.
2. Fear of Airsickness...Barphobia.
1. Fear of Wink Martindale...Tic Tac Doughbia!

10 More Fears And Phobias

10. Fear Of Star Wars...Obee Won Kenobia.
9. Fear Of Ron Howard...Opeibia.
8. Fear Of Saturday Night Live...Don Pardobia.
7. Fear Of Making Too Many Appearances On The Love Boat...Charobia.
6. Fear Of The Rolling Stones...Can't Get Nobia.
5. Fear Of Committing A Crime And Getting Caught...Columbobia.
4. Fear Of The Circus...Dumbobia.
3. Fear Of Breakfast...Cheeriobia.
2. Fear Of Sleeping With The Fishes...Angelo Brunobia.
1. Fear Of Boyscouts...Webelobia.

The Media

If it weren't for the media, I wouldn't have a job. No kidding, duh! Everyone loves TV and music. There were scores of lists about this subject. Here are five that still make me scream!

10 Jewish Elvis Songs

10. Jail House Lox
9. Love Me Torah
8. Blue Chawaii
7. Blue Suede Sofa
6. Oy Vey Mama
5. Cryin' In The Temple
4. Return To Sendberg
3. Are You Kosher Tonight?
2. Ya Way
1. Viva Las Bagels

10 Dwarfs That Didn't Make The Final Seven

10. The Promiscuous Dwarf...Easy
9. The Dwarf With PMS...Crampy
8. The Dwarf From The Jeffersons...Wheezy
7. The Dwarf Who Banged Snow White...Lucky
6. The Dwarf Who Plays With Chain Saws...Stumpy
5. The Dwarf Who Owns The 7-11...Sengi
4. The Dwarf Who Walks On Franklin St....Skanky
3. The Incontinent Dwarf...Smelly
2. The Rat Pack Dwarf...Sammy
1. The Really Well Hung Dwarf...Meat

10 Names For Angela Lansbury's Less Violent Sequel To Murder, She Wrote

10. Trespassing, She Wrote.
9. Jaywalking, She Wrote.
8. Double Parking, She Wrote.
7. Leaving The Seat Up, She Wrote.
6. Talking To Driver While Bus Is In Motion, She Wrote.
5. Dine And Dash, She Wrote.
4. Tray Not In Upright Position While Landing, She Wrote.
3. Farting In Elevator, She Wrote.
2. Ripping The Tag Off The Mattress, She Wrote.
1. Rebroadcasting, Reaccounting And Retransmitting A Game Without The Expressed Consent Of Major League Baseball, She Wrote.

Remember this billboard? Who came up with this? It wasn't me!

10 Bad Charlie Brown Episodes

10. It's The Great Wall Of China, Charlie Brown!
9. You're Queer, Charlie Brown!
8. Your Dog's Humping My Leg, Charlie Brown!
7. Thumbs Ain't The Only Thing Linus Is Sucking, Charlie Brown!
6. You're Amish, Charlie Brown!
5. It's A Charlie Brown Yom Kippur!
4. Throw The Guy A Change Up, Charlie Brown!
3. You're Not Just The Hair Club President, Charlie Brown!
2. Lucy's A Bitch, Charlie Brown!
1. Peppermint Patti Is Dealing Some Bad Dust, Charlie Brown!

10 TV Shows That Didn't Quite Make It

10. The cartoon bird who was a real jerk...The Woody Peckerhead Show.
9. Mr. Greenjeans goes to the "hood"...Captain Gangaroo.
8. Melissa Gilbert isn't so innocent...Little Ho On The Prairie.
7. Ricky's little secret comes out...I Love Louie.
6. How to save your lawn...Fescue 911.
5. An organ donor becomes a farmer...Spleen Acres.
4. Game shows of Ancient Romans...To Tell The TRVTH.
3. Major Nelson spends a little too much time with Major Healy...I Dream Of Gene.
2. An English professor takes over successful HBO sitcom...On Dream (get it?)
1. Teenage doctor becomes adult film star...Doogie Howitzer.

New York Post Headlines

One of my favorite topics for the list is what I call, "Famous Moments in History and How They Would Be Reported in the New York Post." The Post is that tabloid daily that sort of condenses the headline into something quite mundane. Example? If the Yankees would take the World Series, the headline would read, "WE WIN!"

10 Moments In History And How They Would Be Reported In The New York Post

10. Near Meltdown At TMI: Headline Reads…"Well Done Harrisburgers."
9. Japan Surrenders: Headline Reads…"No Go Tojo!"
8. November 22, 1963: Headline Reads…"JF KO'd!"
7. Gandhi Leads India: Headline Reads…"Slurpees For Everyone!"
6. U.S Warship Vincennes Shoots Down Iranian Jetliner: Headline Reads…."Whoomp There It Is!"
5. First Man On Moon: Headline Reads…"It's Not Cheese!"
4. Alexander Graham Bell Invents Telephone. Headline Reads…"It's For You!"
3. Reagan Shot. Headline Reads…"Hinckley Misses!"
2. 1989 Bay Area Earthquake. Headline Reads…"Crack Opens In Frisco!"
1. Christ Is Born. Headline Reads…"No More Shopping Days."

10 More Moments In History And How They Would Be Reported In The New York Post

10. Cuban Missile Crisis. Headline Reads…"Castrated."
9. Hawaii Finally Admitted As A State. Headline Reads…"Book 'em Dano."

8. Mike Browne Loses Virginity. Headline Reads…"Hey Mikey. He Likes It!"
7. Big Fire At The Old Gray Iron Castings Building In Reading. Headline Reads…"Hot Enough For Ya?"
6. Land Purchased From American Indians. Headline Reads…"What, No Coupon?"
5. Hurricane Agnes Floods Birdsboro. Headline Reads…"Hey, Bath Night Ain't Until Saturday!"
4. Old Pomeroy's Building Torn Down. Headline Reads…"Bon Ton Gone Gone!"
3. Simpson Chased In White Ford Bronco. Headline Reads…"O.J. Can You Flee?"
2. Hugh Grant Arrested With Prostitute. Headline Reads…"Heads Up Hugh."
1. Nixon Resigns. Headline Reads…"No More Dick!"

The fellas along with State Representative Dante Santoni and Tim Smith, Legislative Aid to Congressman Tim Holden, at the Mike & Dave Seventh Anniversary Party.

10 More Moments In History And How They Would Be Reported In The New York Post

10. John DuPont Arrested After Killing Wrestler. Headline Reads..."Teflon Does Stick."
9. Big Blizzard Hits The East Coast. Headline Reads..."Maier's Breaks Sales Records."
8. Pope Visits Meadowlands. Headline Reads..."Drop Back And Pontiff!"
7. Blue Angels Come To Reading. Headline Reads..."Mike Pukes."
6. Saturday Night Live Cast Axed. Headline Reads..."Buh Bye."
5. Phils Third Baseman Retires. Headline Reads..."Oh Schmidt!"
4. Thornburgh Elected Governor. Headline Reads..."Just Another Dick In Harrisburg."
3. Wilt Chamberlain Has Sex For The First Time. Headline Reads..."24,999 To Go!"
2. Y-102 Goes Rock Hits. Headline Reads..."Bye-Bye Bolton."
1. Hugh Grant Busted With Hooker. Headline Reads..."Who's The Ho Hugh?"

Last Part

Another big night at The Reading Comedy Outlet with Raymond!

Mike and Dave, circa 1996.

The voice you hear laughing in the background during the 7:20 List is our WRAW newscaster, Sue Sheetz. You may have noticed she wasn't around for a while. Sue learned she had a benign brain tumor earlier this year. After surgery and a remarkable recovery, Sue is back to work and laughing like always. We are so very happy she is back.

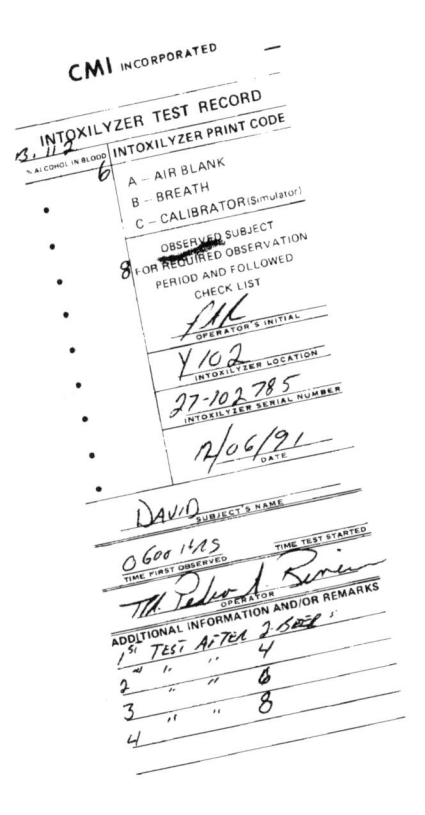

Remember when the State Police came in and did an on-air drinking and driving test on me? Here is my intoxilyzer test after 8 beers. I normally do not drink more than a couple. I was loopy!

FIREHOUSE
BAR AND RESTAURANT

2nd and Penn Streets
(794 Feet from the West Shore Bypass)

Like I don't have enough to do. David Stein's Firehouse Bar & Restaurant is something of a dream come true for me. I hope you'll enjoy it as much as I do.

And finally:

10 Things Overheard At Y-102 In February Of 1988

10. Well, at least they won't be here next year.
9. Who's the geek with the mustache?
8. They said what?!?
7. Mike, some girl's on the phone for you.
6. This ain't L.A., fellas.
5. You can't say "ass."
4. It won't work in Berks County.
3. Don't quit your day job.
2. You suck.
1. It'll never last.

Not really funny, but it's my club, and I get as much stage time as I want at The Reading Comedy Outlet.

WYOMISSING, PENNSYLVANIA 19610

February 19, 1988

Manager
WRFY-FM
1265 Perkiomen Avenue
Reading, Pennsylvania 19602

Dear Sir:

    I had the distinctly distasteful experience of having tuned in the morning program on WRFY-FM this morning. The scenarios I heard rank among the worst of the murky depths of British humor. I do not ever want to hear another song about a woman passing gas through her jeans on your station again. I was also very definitely offended by the jokes propagated on the premise of a man mating with a gorilla.

    This is disgusting and totally distasteful. I will not tolerate this type of programming in Reading, Pennsylvania. You can rest assured that if you cannot clean up the humor on your radio station, I will do everything in my power to get your station off the air. If you think that this is a hollow threat, watch me.

                                Sincerely,

Excerpt of a letter we received FOUR DAYS after the Morning Show Began!